Elements

MATT MULLINS

Children's Press®
An Imprint of Scholastic Inc.
New York Toronto London Auckland Sydney
Mexico City New Delhi Hong Kong
Danbury, Connecticut

Content Consultant
Suzanne E. Willis
Professor and Assistant Chair, Department of Physics
Northern Illinois University
DeKalb, Illinois

Library of Congress Cataloging-in-Publication Data

Mullins, Matt.
　The Elements/Matt Mullins.
　　p. cm.—(A true book)
　Includes bibliographical references and index.
　ISBN-13: 978-0-531-26323-5 (lib. bdg.)　　　ISBN-10: 0-531-26323-1 (lib. bdg.)
　ISBN-13: 978-0-531-26585-7 (pbk.)　　　　　ISBN-10: 0-531-26585-4 (pbk.)
　1. Periodic law—Tables—Juvenile literature. 2. Chemical
elements—Juvenile literature. I. Title. II. Series.
　QD467.M85 2012
　546'.8—dc22

　　　　　　　　　　　　　　　　　　　　　　2011010400

All rights reserved. Published in 2012 by Children's Press, an imprint of Scholastic Inc.
Printed in China 62
SCHOLASTIC, CHILDREN'S PRESS, A TRUE BOOK, and associated logos are trademarks and/or registered trademarks of Scholastic Inc.
1 2 3 4 5 6 7 8 9 10 R 21 20 19 18 17 16 15 14 13 12

Find the Truth!

Everything you are about to read is true *except* for one of the sentences on this page.

Which one is **TRUE**?

T or F   The periodic table describes every known element.

T or F   Atomic mass and atomic number are the same thing.

Find the answers in this book. ➡

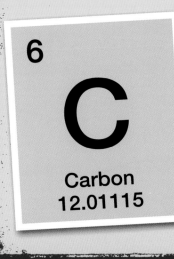

6

C

Carbon
12.01115

Contents

THE **BIG** TRUTH!

The Periodic Table

The element helium makes
balloons float.

A water molecule

3 Using the Table

What is the role of electrons in the formation of matter? **29**

4 Combining Elements

How do elements combine with other elements? **37**

Hydrogen is the most common element in the universe.

5

Chemists study matter.

CHAPTER 1

Chemistry Organizes Matter

What do you think a chemist looks like? Do you picture someone wearing a long, white laboratory coat? Maybe this person is surrounded by strange-looking containers with boiling, colored liquids in them. If you see a chemist who looks like this, he or she is working with matter.

 Chemistry is often called the "central science."

Matter Matters

Chemistry is the science of substances. Substances are matter. Everything is made of matter. A tiny speck of dust is matter. A distant star is made from matter. The air we breathe is matter. People are made of matter. All matter is made of **atoms**, the tiniest, most basic portion of any kind of matter. Most of the time, matter is made from several different kinds of atoms that are joined together.

Our entire universe is made up of matter.

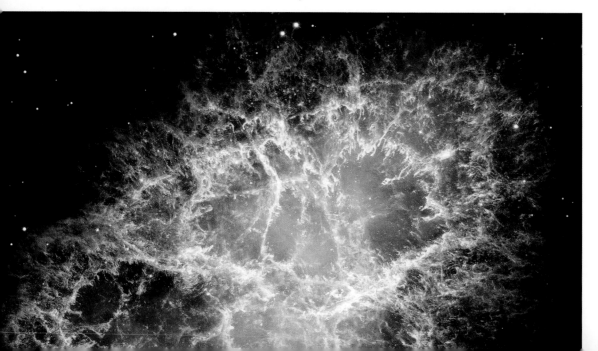

Water, for example, is a combination of two hydrogen atoms and one oxygen atom. A chemist would write that combination as H_2O. Hydrogen and oxygen are called **elements**. Elements are the basic building blocks of all matter. They cannot be split into simpler substances. The atoms of each element are identical to one another—and different from the atoms of every other element.

John Dalton's discoveries had a major impact on scientists' knowledge of matter.

John Dalton proposed the "atomic theory of matter" in 1803.

Scientists have experimented with matter for hundreds of years.

The Periodic Table

Some elements are similar to others. For that reason, scientists think of elements as belonging to different groups, or families. To help organize the elements into these different groups, we use a special chart. The chart is called the periodic table, and it provides important information about every known element.

The periodic table is also called the "periodic table of the chemical elements." It shows the atomic **mass,** or weight, of each element. The table assigns each element an **atomic number** which gives us important information about that element. The periodic table also arranges elements that have common properties into "families."

The periodic table is sometimes called the bible of chemistry.

Periodic Table of the Elements

Chemistry Gets Organized

Chemistry became more organized when the periodic table was accepted by scientists. Chemists began discovering new elements. They observed connections between elements that had not been seen before. The periodic table also helps scientists to determine if elements will combine easily. It is one of a scientist's most practical and useful tools.

Chemists experiment to find out how different elements affect each other.

Sometimes we use chemicals to separate an element from a combination of elements. The periodic table helps us understand how we can separate elements. The table helps us determine how things in the natural world are made. We also learn how to combine elements into things that do not occur in nature. The periodic table helps scientists create products such as medicines, plastics, food flavorings, and much more.

Some elements can cause interesting results when they are mixed together.

The elements found on Earth are also found throughout the universe.

Ancient Greek philosophers considered
fire one of four main elements.

CHAPTER 2

Building the Periodic Table

People have wondered about matter for a long time. In the fourth century B.C.E., the Greek philosopher Aristotle (AYR-ih-stot-uhl) had an idea. He suggested that all matter on Earth was a mixture of four basic elements: earth, water, air, and fire. A log, for instance, was made of these four elements. When the log was burned, the elements separated into ash, smoke, and bubbling sap.

Aristotle believed that a fifth element, called ether, filled space.

A New View

For almost 2,000 years, scientists believed that all matter was made from those four basic elements. In 1661, however, English scientist Robert Boyle noticed something. No one had ever pulled any of Aristotle's four elements out of a mixture. Boyle argued there must be simple, basic pieces from which matter is made. These "pieces" later became known as atoms.

Robert Boyle contributed important information to several branches of science.

Scientists had identified about a dozen elements, such as gold and mercury, before Boyle published his ideas. More discoveries followed. In 1669, Hennig Brand, a German chemist, was trying to make gold from other matter. He didn't make gold, but he did discover the element phosphorus. Several years later, Boyle found a way to isolate pure phosphorus from a compound. Other elements— such as cobalt, platinum, hydrogen, oxygen, and chlorine— were soon discovered.

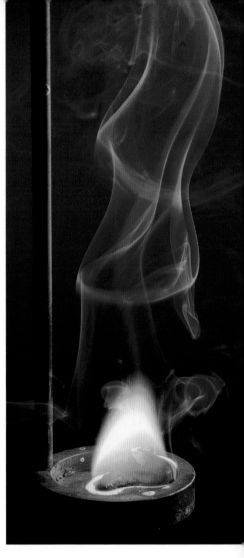

Phosphorus glows in the dark at room temperature.

Hennig Brand discovered phosphorus by boiling urine.

Robert Boyle called the basic pieces of matter corpuscles.

The establishment of chemistry departments in universities led to more young scientists studying matter.

Chemistry Grows Up

Fifty more elements were discovered in the 200 years after Boyle published his ideas. Some of these elements were metals. Others were nonmetals, and some were gases. Scientists began to gather more and more information on elements. Chemists began to wonder how to organize them. Chemistry became a more important science. Universities began to offer chemistry classes.

Trying to Make Gold

For hundreds of years, chemistry developed through a craft called alchemy. Alchemists tried to solve two problems. One was to make gold from less expensive matter. The other was to find a potion that would give long life. Chemistry developed out of the work of alchemists. Several important scientists, such as Sir Isaac Newton, were alchemists. Newton changed the way we think about our world by defining the laws of motion and gravity.

The Birth of the Periodic Table

In 1869, Russian chemist Dmitri Mendeleev was preparing to teach a class in chemistry. He began to organize information on elements, focusing on their weight. Mendeleev organized 57 known elements on a chart. He listed them in order of their weight. Each element had a different weight. He noticed that elements known to be similar seemed to be grouping together on his chart.

Dmitri Mendeleev published more than 400 books and articles during his career.

Mendeleev was not the first scientist to arrange elements in a chart. But his chart was special. It was well organized and left spaces where newly discovered elements could be added. For instance, Mendeleev left a space between chlorine and potassium. He noticed that there was a weight between those two elements that no known element had. In 1894, Sir William Ramsay identified a gas that had the missing weight: argon.

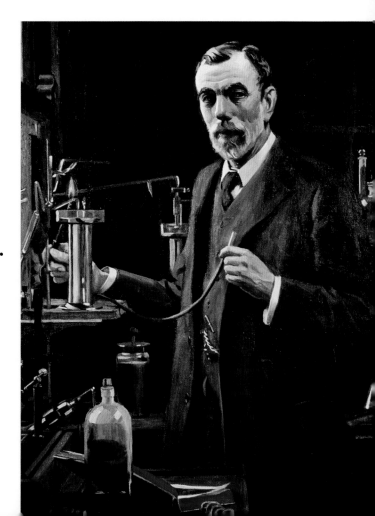

Sir William Ramsay won the 1904 Nobel Prize in Chemistry.

Periods and Groups

Mendeleev's table is organized into horizontal rows, called periods. The table also has vertical columns, called groups. Each group of elements has similar physical qualities and chemical behavior. This arrangement allows scientists to discover new elements and place them on the table. In 1895, Ramsay proved the existence of helium, located right after hydrogen in the table's first period.

Helium was first detected in 1868 by scientists studying light from the sun.

The element neon is used to create glowing signs.

In the following century, 41 more elements were found. In 1898, Ramsay used the periodic table when he discovered the gas neon. He predicted from a version of Mendeleev's table that three more gases similar to argon and helium would be found. Ramsay soon found krypton, neon, and xenon.

The atomic nucleus was discovered by Ernest Rutherford in 1911.

Ernest Rutherford won the Nobel Prize in Chemistry in 1908.

Improvements

Mendeleev's table did not work perfectly in all cases. The arrangement of elements by weight occasionally put elements together in odd ways. In the early 1900s, scientists discovered that each atom's **nucleus** contained **protons**. These little particles were balanced out by **electrons** circling around the nucleus. Scientists decided to organize the elements by **atomic number**, or the number of protons in each element. They discovered that the number of protons was a better way to predict relationships between elements than weight.

Since this rearrangement of the table by atomic number, more elements have been discovered. As of 2011, there were 118 elements on the periodic table. It isn't arranged by weight but it still looks a lot like it did when Mendeleev was preparing to teach his students.

Students and chemists today use an updated version of the periodic table.

The Periodic Table

In the early 1900s, scientists rearranged Mendeleev's table. The new table is the one we currently use. It lists elements according to their atomic number. The atomic number is the number of protons in an element's nucleus. This is a more accurate way to arrange elements and to find missing ones. The new arrangement also helps scientists understand what elements could join easily with other elements.

The atomic number indicates how many protons the element has.

This is the symbol, or abbreviation, for the element.

6
C
Carbon
12.01115

This is the name of the element.

The atomic mass indicates the mass, or weight, of the atom of the element.

Periodic Table of the Elements

Legend	
Metals	Transition Elements	Inner Transition Elements
Nonmetals	Noble Gases	★ Synthetic
		▲ Radioactive

1 New designation
1A Original designation

( ) Atomic weight of most stable isotope

Period 1
1 1A — **H** Hydrogen 1.00797
18 8A — 2 **He** Helium 4.0026

Period 2 — 3 **Li** Lithium 6.941 — 4 **Be** Beryllium 9.0122 — 5 **B** Boron 10.811 — 6 **C** Carbon 12.01115 — 7 **N** Nitrogen 14.0067 — 8 **O** Oxygen 15.9994 — 9 **F** Fluorine 8.9984 — 10 **Ne** Neon 20.179

Period 3 — 11 **Na** Sodium 22.9896 — 12 **Mg** Magnesium 24.305 — 13 **Al** Aluminum 26.9815 — 14 **Si** Silicon 28.086 — 15 **P** Phosphorus 30.9738 — 16 **S** Sulfur 32.064 — 17 **Cl** Chlorine 35.453 — 18 **Ar** Argon 39.948

Period 4 — 19 **K** Potassium 39.0983 — 20 **Ca** Calcium 40.08 — 21 **Sc** Scandium 44.956 — 22 **Ti** Titanium 47.88 — 23 **V** Vanadium 50.942 — 24 **Cr** Chromium 51.996 — 25 **Mn** Manganese 54.9380 — 26 **Fe** Iron 55.847 — 27 **Co** Cobalt 58.9332 — 28 **Ni** Nickel 58.69 — 29 **Cu** Copper 63.54 — 30 **Zn** Zinc 65.37 — 31 **Ga** Gallium 69.72 — 32 **Ge** Germanium 72.59 — 33 **As** Arsenic 74.9216 — 34 **Se** Selenium 78.96 — 35 **Br** Bromine 79.904 — 36 **Kr** Krypton 83.80

Period 5 — 37 **Rb** Rubidium 85.4678 — 38 **Sr** Strontium 87.62 — 39 **Y** Yttrium 88.906 — 40 **Zr** Zirconium 91.22 — 41 **Nb** Niobium 92.906 — 42 **Mo** Molybdenum 95.94 — 43 **Tc** Technetium (98) — 44 **Ru** Ruthenium 101.07 — 45 **Rh** Rhodium 102.906 — 46 **Pd** Palladium 106.4 — 47 **Ag** Silver 107.868 — 48 **Cd** Cadmium 112.40 — 49 **In** Indium 114.82 — 50 **Sn** Tin 118.69 — 51 **Sb** Antimony 121.75 — 52 **Te** Tellurium 127.60 — 53 **I** Iodine 126.9044 — 54 **Xe** Xenon 131.29

Period 6 — 55 **Cs** Cesium 132.905 — 56 **Ba** Barium 137.33 — 72 **Hf** Hafnium 178.49 — 73 **Ta** Tantalum 180.948 — 74 **W** Tungsten 183.85 — 75 **Re** Rhenium 186.2 — 76 **Os** Osmium 190.2 — 77 **Ir** Iridium 192.2 — 78 **Pt** Platinum 195.09 — 79 **Au** Gold 196.967 — 80 **Hg** Mercury 200.59 — 81 **Tl** Thallium 204.383 — 82 **Pb** Lead 207.19 — 83 **Bi** Bismuth 208.980 — 84 **Po** Polonium (209) — 85 **At** Astatine (210) — 86 **Rn** Radon (222)

Period 7 — 87 **Fr** Francium (223) — 88 **Ra** Radium (226.0254) — 104 **Rf** Rutherfordium (261) — 105 **Db** Dubnium (262) — 106 **Sg** Seaborgium (263) — 107 **Bh** Bohrium (262) — 108 **Hs** Hassium (265) — 109 **Mt** Meitnerium (266) — 110 **Ds** Darmstadtium (269) — 111 **Rg** Roentgenium (272) — 112 **Uub** Ununbium (277) — 113 **Uut** — 114 **Uuq** — 115 **Uup** — 116 **Uuh** — 117 **Uus** — 118 **Uuo**

Unknown elements 113 - 118 are shown in their predicted positions.

Lanthanide Series 6 — 57 **La** Lanthanum 138.91 — 58 **Ce** Cerium 140.12 — 59 **Pr** Praseodymium 140.907 — 60 **Nd** Neodymium 144.24 — 61 **Pm** Promethium (146) — 62 **Sm** Samarium 150.35 — 63 **Eu** Europium 151.96 — 64 **Gd** Gadolinium 157.25 — 65 **Tb** Terbium 158.9254 — 66 **Dy** Dysprosium 162.50 — 67 **Ho** Holmium 164.930 — 68 **Er** Erbium 167.26 — 69 **Tm** Thulium 168.934 — 70 **Yb** Ytterbium 173.04 — 71 **Lu** Lutetium 174.97

Actinide Series 7 — 89 **Ac** Actinium (227.0278) — 90 **Th** Thorium 232.038 — 91 **Pa** Protactinium (231.0359) — 92 **U** Uranium 238.03 — 93 **Np** Neptunium (237.0482) — 94 **Pu** Plutonium (244) — 95 **Am** Americium (243) — 96 **Cm** Curium (247) — 97 **Bk** Berkelium (249) — 98 **Cf** Californium (251) — 99 **Es** Einsteinium (252) — 100 **Fm** Fermium (257) — 101 **Md** Mendelevium (258) — 102 **No** Nobelium (259) — 103 **Lr** Lawrencium (260)

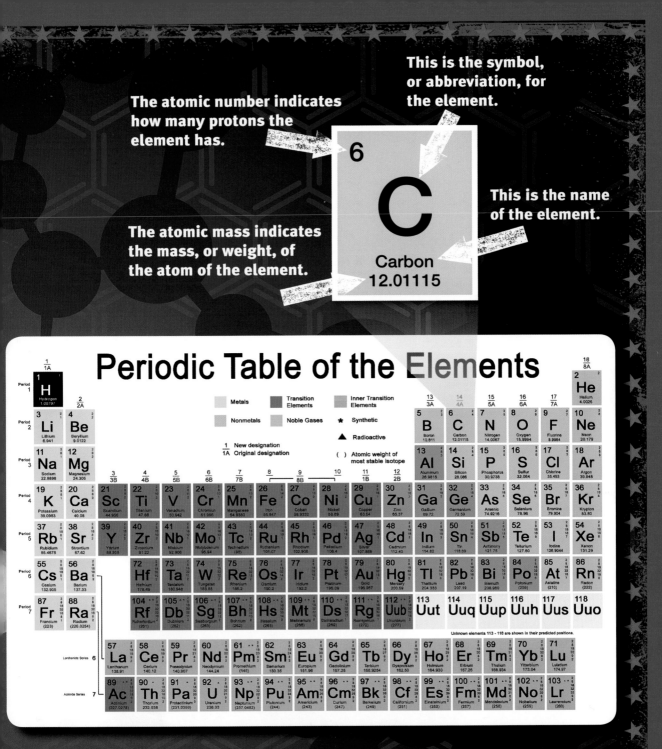

The periodic table makes it easy for young scientists to understand how elements relate to each other.

Be
4

B
10.81

V 23	Cr 24	Mn 25	Fe 26	Co 27	Ni 28
50.9415	51.996	54.9380	55.847	58.9332	58.69
Nb 41	Mo 42	Tc 43	Ru 44	Rh 45	Pd 46
92.9064	95.94	(98)	101.07	102.9055	106.42
Ta 73	W 74	Re 75	Os 76	Ir 77	Pt 78
180.9479	183.85	186.207	190.2	192.22	
Ha 105	Sg 106	Uns 107	Uno 108		
(262)	(263)	(262)			

Hf 72
178.49

Rf 104

Ce 57/58	Pr 59	N
140.12	140.9077	

90
h Pa
Nb

28

CHAPTER 3

Using the Table

Each small box on the periodic table is packed with important information. Each box includes the symbol, or abbreviation, for the element. It also contains the element's name, the atomic number, and the atomic mass. This simple arrangement of information can tell us what the atom of each element looks like.

Potassium, symbolized by K on the periodic table, will burst into flame if it is dropped into water.

| 19 |
| K |
| Potassium |
| 39.0983 |

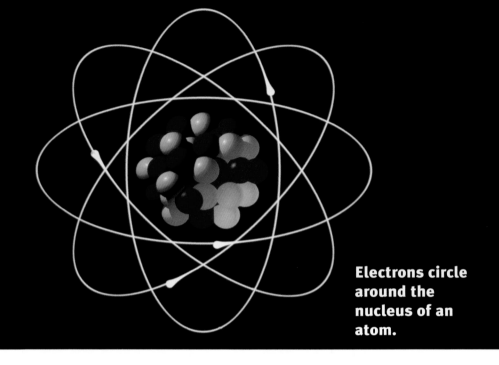

Electrons circle around the nucleus of an atom.

Electrons

For each proton in the nucleus of an atom, there is an electron circling the nucleus. For example, hydrogen has one proton, so it has one electron.

Electrons circle in different levels around the nucleus. Each level is like a round shell. Electrons circle in up to three shells in lighter elements. The first shell can hold two electrons, the second eight more electrons, and the third 18 after that.

 Negative electrical charges give electrons their name.

The periodic table indicates more than just how many electrons each element has. It even indicates how many electrons circle in the outermost shell. Later, we will see why it is useful to know how many electrons rotate in the outer shell.

Scientists build large machines called particle accelerators to help them study atoms.

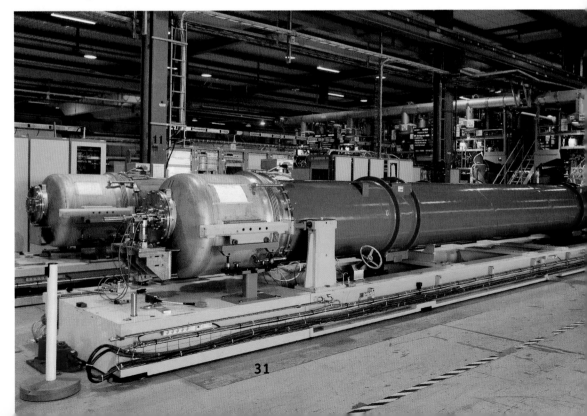

31

Take a look at the periodic table on page 27. As you move along each row, or period, you will notice that the atomic number increases by one. Hydrogen (H), atomic number 1, has one electron rotating around the nucleus. It rotates in the first shell. Helium (He) has two electrons. They both rotate in the first shell. These are both in the first row, so they are called Period 1.

Helium makes balloons float because it is lighter than Earth's air.

Lithium is light enough to float on water. →

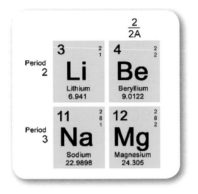

Period 2 begins with lithium (Li), which has three electrons: two in the first shell and one in the second. Neon (Ne), at the end of Period 2, has 10 electrons: two in the first shell and eight in the second. Sodium (Na) has an atomic number of 11, and starts Period 3. It has two electrons in the first shell, eight in the second, and one in the third.

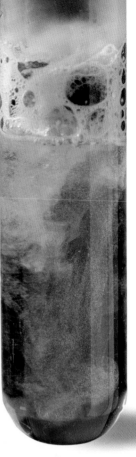

Lithium produces hydrogen gas when it mixes with water.

Now look at each column, or group. They are labeled 1 through 18. Elements in the same group have similar properties. For example, hydrogen, lithium, and sodium are in Group 1. They all have one electron in the outer shell.

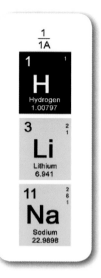

Timeline of the Periodic Table

300s B.C.

Aristotle suggests everything on Earth is composed from four elements: earth, water, air, and fire.

1661

Robert Boyle argues against Aristotle's theory.

Atomic Mass

The atomic mass of each element is the number at the bottom of each element's square. The atomic mass is how much stuff is in the element. It is the element's weight. Knowing the atomic mass helps scientists when they work with combinations of elements.

1669

Hennig Brand discovers phosphorus, the first scientifically discovered element.

1869

Mendeleev creates a periodic table of elements ordered by weight.

The element sodium doesn't look anything like table salt, but it becomes salt when it combines with chlorine.

CHAPTER 4

Combining Elements

Now we know how atoms are structured. We still need to learn how elements combine with other elements. In water, two atoms of hydrogen bind with one atom of oxygen. Sodium chloride is created when one atom of sodium binds with one atom of chlorine. You know this **compound** as common table salt. Before the elements combine, none of them look like water or salt. Oxygen, hydrogen, and chlorine are gases. Sodium is a soft, silvery metal.

When multiple elements bind together, they create a compound.

Electrons at Work

Compounds are found everywhere. They exist because elements combine. Atoms need to have full outer shells to stay stable. If the outer shell is not full, the atom may try to fill the shell. Some atoms are missing an electron or two to make up a full shell. Others have one or two extra electrons outside a full shell. If these atoms share their electrons, they can both have full outer shells.

When viewed up close, grains of sugar look like rocks.

Sugar is made of carbon, hydrogen, and oxygen.

Smaller Than an Atom

There are smaller things than atoms. Protons, electrons, and **neutrons** are smaller, of course. But even these tiny particles have smaller particles inside them. Scientists have found gluons and quarks inside protons and neutrons.

39

A **molecule** is two or more atoms joined together. For example, a water molecule takes advantage of outer-shell incompleteness. Oxygen has an atomic number of eight. It has two electrons in its full first shell. It has only six in its second shell. It would be complete with eight in that outer shell. Hydrogen is complete with its one electron in its one shell. But when two hydrogens meet up with one oxygen, what occurs?

A water molecule is made up of two hydrogen atoms and one oxygen atom.

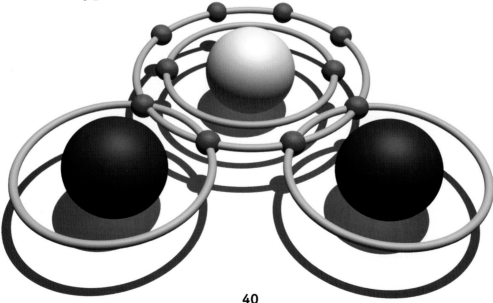

Water is one of the most common compounds on Earth.

Water is one of the compounds our bodies need in order for us to live.

The two hydrogens link to oxygen. These two single-shell electrons connect to the outer shell of oxygen. This gives oxygen a complete shell of eight electrons. The hydrogen atoms attach to the oxygen in a way that gives their shell two electrons. Table salt is also a compound. But the sodium and chlorine combine in a different way than hydrogen and oxygen do to form water. The atomic numbers on the periodic table tell us why.

Sodium and chlorine combine into cube-shaped molecules called crystals.

Sodium has only one electron in its nearly empty outer shell (it is in Group 1). It donates this electron to chlorine, which has seven electrons in its outer shell (Group 7). Sodium becomes complete with one less electron and two full shells. Chlorine gets a full outer shell. The result is salt.

Scientists continue to find new compounds. There are still many new things to discover about elements! ★

Number of elements in Dmitri Mendeleev's first periodic table: 57

Number of elements in the periodic table today: 118

Electrical charge of a proton: +1

Electrical charge of an electron: −1

Atomic weight of ununoctium, the heaviest element on the periodic table: 294

Most common element in the universe: Hydrogen

Number of people to win a Nobel Prize in Chemistry by 2010: 159

Number of votes Mendeleev fell short of winning a Nobel Prize in Chemistry: 1

Diameter of a hydrogen atom: 1/10,000,000 mm

Did you find the truth?

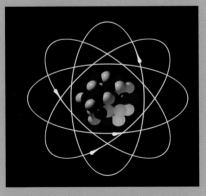

T The periodic table describes every known element.

F Atomic mass and atomic number are the same thing.

Resources

Books

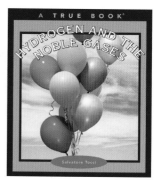

Basher, Simon, and Adrian Dingle. *The Periodic Table: Elements With Style!* New York: Kingfisher, 2007.

Basher, Simon, and Dan Green. *Chemistry: Getting a Big Reaction!* New York: Kingfisher, 2010.

Bradley, David. *Atoms and Elements*. New York: Oxford University Press, 2002.

Saucerman, Linda. *Hydrogen: Understanding the Elements of the Periodic Table*. New York: Rosen, 2004.

Tocci, Salvatore. *Hydrogen and the Noble Gases*. New York: Children's Press, 2004.

Woodford, Chris. *Potassium*. New York: Benchmark Books, 2002.

Zannos, Susan. *Dmitri Mendeleyev and the Periodic Table*. Hockessin, DE: Mitchell Lane, 2004.

Organizations and Web Sites

Chem4Kids.com — Periodic Table and the Elements
www.chem4kids.com/files/elem_intro.html
Learn about elements, atoms, the periodic table, and more.

AIP Center for the History of Physics — Marie Curie and the Science of Radioactivity
www.aip.org/history/curie
Learn all about physicist and chemist Marie Curie — her life and her many discoveries.

Museum of the Periodic Table (Online)
http://ptable.freediscovery.com/index.html
View quick online exhibits, read the history, and see news and information on the elements.

Places to Visit

American Museum of Natural History
Central Park West at 79th Street
New York, NY 10024
(212) 769-5100
www.amnh.org
See exhibits on famous chemists, their discoveries, and more.

Harvard Museum of Natural History
26 Oxford Street
Cambridge, MA 02138
(617) 495-3045
www.hmnh.harvard.edu
View minerals organized by chemical element composition.

Important Words

atoms (AT-uhmz)—the tiniest parts of an element that have all the properties of that element

atomic number (uh-TOM-ik NUM-buhr)—the number of protons in the nucleus of an atom of a chemical element

chemistry (KEM-i-stree)—the scientific study of substances, their composition, and how they react with each other

compound (KAHM-pound)—a substance made from two or more chemical elements

electrons (i-LEK-trahnz)—tiny negatively charged particles that move around the nucleus of an atom

elements (EL-uh-muhntz)—substances that cannot be divided up into simpler substances

mass (MAS)—the physical matter that an object contains; its weight

molecule (MAH-luh-kyool)—the smallest unit that a chemical compound can be divided into that still displays all of its chemical properties

neutrons (NOO-trahnz)—particles inside a nucleus, similar to protons but with no electrical charge

nucleus (NOO-klee-uhs) — the central part of an atom that is made up of neutrons and protons

protons (PROH-tahnz) — positively charged particles inside a nucleus

Index

Page numbers in **bold** indicate illustrations

About the Author

Matt Mullins holds a master's degree in the history of science from the University of Wisconsin–Madison. Formerly a newspaper reporter, Matt has been a science writer and research consultant for nine years. Matt has written more than two dozen children's books, and has written and directed a few short films. He lives in Madison with his son.